WAVE

SPLAT

A CALL FOR A NEW ALPHABET

Jef Czekaj

📖 Charlesbridge

It was an average day in Alphabet City.
S was soaking up some sun, bearded B
was bouncing a ball, R was roller-skating,
and there was P in the pool.

Every letter was happy and content.

Every letter, that is, except for X.
X was excited and exasperated.

Helpful H explained.

That's the way it's always been.

The alphabet always starts with A, then comes B, then C, all the way to Z.

See, you're **way** down here.

The alphabet needs order, just like grammar needs rules.

Well, I'm SICK of all these rules!

X caused quite a commotion. Never before had someone suggested that the alphabet be altered. The confused letters gathered to listen to X's explosive words.

The letters were at odds over X's ideas.

Y was yelling at W.

S was sobbing.

R was ranting at T.

The alphabet seemed to be falling apart
when suddenly . . .

The letters cheered.

That night X was so excited that he could barely sleep.

Eventually he drifted off to sleep, where he had the strangest dreams.

First he dreamed that he was S. He ran from word to word, finding that most words became plural—meaning more than one of something—with the addition of an S at the end.

Of course, there were exceptions.

As X charged up the stairs of Alphabet Hall,
he heard the voice of Judge J.

A hush fell over the crowd. If X's vote was a "yes," the alphabet that we all learned in school would be thrown out.

My distinguished consonants and vowels. I stand before you to humbly cast my vote.

Yesterday I was **sure** we needed a new alphabet. I was sick of my lowly role and jealous of all the other letters.

Needless to say, the alphabet was shocked and reacted in many unique ways.

G gasped.

B breathed a sigh of relief.

O offered his opinions.

F fainted.

J jumped for joy.

R, for some reason, roller-skated away.

And so it was that the alphabet remained as it has been since you and I were young. X proudly took his place third to last in the alphabet.

Y was also happy to be back where she belonged.

sky

yacht

yo-yo

Ah, it's great to have everything back to normal. Isn't that right, Z? Z? Z?

Z was snoozing. It had been a very, very long couple of days.

for

Published by Charlesbridge
85 Main Street
Watertown, MA 02472
(617) 926-0329
www.charlesbridge.com

Library of Congress Cataloging-in-Publication Data
Czekaj, Jef.
  A call for a new alphabet / Jef Czekaj.
    p. cm.
  Summary: Tired of being near the end of the alphabet, starting few words, and being
governed by grammar rules, X calls for a vote on a new Alphabet Constitution, then
dreams of how life would be if he became a different letter.
  ISBN 978-1-58089-228-5 (reinforced for library use)
  ISBN 978-1-58089-229-2 (softcover)
[1. Alphabet—Fiction. 2. English language—Grammar—Fiction. 3. Voting—Fiction.
4. Humorous stories.] I. Title.
PZ7.C9987Cal 2011
[E]—dc22   2010007534

Printed in Singapore
(hc) 10 9 8 7 6 5 4 3 2 1
(sc) 10 9 8 7 6 5 4 3 2 1

Line art drawn in ink on Bristol paper and then scanned and colored
  on a MacBook Pro using Adobe Photoshop
Display type and text type set in EyeCheck and Cheltenham
Color separations by Chroma Graphics, Singapore
Printed and bound September 2010 by Imago in Singapore
Production supervision by Brian G. Walker
Designed by Martha MacLeod Sikkema